*Anne of
Green Gables
Birthday Book*

---

*This Book
Belongs To:*

me

Anne of Green Gables Birthday Book
A Seal Book/April 1990

PRINTING HISTORY

Seal edition

ISBN 0-7704-2362-0

Seal Books are published by McClelland-Bantam, Inc. Its
trademark, consisting of the words "Seal Books" and the portrayal
of a seal, is the property of McClelland-Bantam, Inc., 105 Bond
Street, Toronto, Ontario M5B 1Y3, Canada. This trademark has
been duly registered in the Trademark Office of Canada. The
trademark consisting of the words "Bantam Books" and the
portrayal of a rooster is the property of and is used with the consent
of Bantam Books, 666 Fifth Avenue, New York, New York, 10103.
This trademark has been duly registered in the Trademark Office of
Canada and elsewhere.

Printed and bound in Italy

0 9 8 7 6 5 4 3 2 1

Anne of Green Gables

Birthday Book

Illustrated by Lauren Mills

January

GARNET FOR CONSTANCY

"A few minutes before twelve
Captain Jim rose and opened
the door. 'We must let the
New Year in,' he said."
—*Anne's House of Dreams*

January

1   Simon's

2

3   Christina

4

January

5

6

7

8

9

10

11

12

January

13

14

15

16

January

17
_____
_____
_____

18
_____
_____
_____
_____

19
_____
_____
_____
_____

January

20

21

22

23

January

24

25

26

AUSTRALIA DAY

27

January

28

29

30 Jen

31 Christopher

February

AMETHYST FOR SINCERITY

" 'Diana's birthday is in
February and mine is in
March. Don't you think that is
a very strange coincidence?' "
–*Anne of Green Gables*

February

1

2

3

4

February

5

6

7

8

February

9

10

11

12

February

13 Collete

14

VALENTINE'S DAY

15

16

February

17

18

February

19

20

21   Ben

22

February

23

24

25

26

February

27

28

29
LEAP YEAR

March

BLOODSTONE OR
AQUAMARINE FOR COURAGE

"March came in that winter
like the meekest and mildest
of lambs, bringing days that
were crisp and golden and
tingling. . ."
–Anne of The Island

March

1

2

3

4 Paul
Bud

March

5

6

7

8

March

9

10

11

12

March

13

14 Lizzy

15

16

March

17

ST. PATRICK'S DAY

18

19

20

March

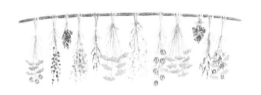

21
_____
_____
_____
_____

22
_____
_____
_____

23
_____
_____
_____
_____

March

24

25

26

27   Dominic

March

28

29

30

31

April

DIAMOND FOR INNOCENCE

"Marilla, walking home one late April evening from an Aid meeting, realized that the winter was over and gone with the thrill of delight that spring never fails to bring..."
–*Anne of Green Gables*

April

1

APRIL FOOL'S DAY

2

3

4

April

5

6

7

8

April

9

10

11

April

12

13

14

15

April

16 micheal

17

18

19

April

20

21 Nonna
James

22

23

April

24

____

25

ANZAC DAY

____

26

____

April

27

28

29

30

May

EMERALD FOR LOVE
AND SUCCESS

"Then, almost before
anybody realized it, spring
had come; out in Avonlea the
Mayflowers were peeping
pinkly out on the sere barrens
where snow-wreaths
lingered..."
–*Anne of Green Gables*

May

1

MAY DAY

2

3

4

May

5

6

7

8

May

9

10

11

12

May

13
_____
_____
_____

14
_____
_____
_____

15
_____
_____
_____

16
_____
_____
_____

May

17

18

19

20

May

21

22

23

May

24
COMMONWEALTH DAY

25

26

27

May

28
_____
_____
_____

29
_____
_____
_____

30
_____
_____

31
_____
_____
_____

June

PEARL, MOONSTONE AND
ALEXANDRITE FOR HEALTH
AND LONGEVITY

"'My birthday is next week,'
said Paul, as they walked up
the long red hill, basking in
the June sunshine . . ."
–*Anne of Avonlea*

June

1

2

3

4

June

5

6

7

8

June

9

10

11

June

12

13

14

15

June

16

17

18

19

June

20

21

22

23

June

24   mom

25

26

June

27

28

29

30

July

RUBY FOR CONTENTMENT

"Anne was sitting at her open
window, for the time forgetful
of the woes of examinations
and the cares of the world, as
she drank in the beauty of the
summer dusk."
–*Anne of Green Gables*

July

1

CANADA DAY

2

3

4

INDEPENDENCE DAY

July

5

6

7 Stacey

8

July

9

10

11

12

July

13

14

15

16

July

17

18

19

July

20

21

22

23

July

24
_____
_____
_____

25
_____
_____
_____
_____

26
_____
_____
_____

27
_____
_____
_____
_____

July

28

29

30

31

August

SARDONYX AND PERIDOT
FOR MARRIED HAPPINESS

" 'Oh, Marilla,' she exclaimed
breathlessly, 'there's going to
be a Sunday school picnic
next week—in Mr. Harmon
Andrews' field, right near the
Lake of Shining Waters.' "
–*Anne of Green Gables*

August

1

2

3

4

August

5 Dad
Kelley
Jaime

6

7

8

August

9

10

11

12 Petie & Timmy

August

13

14

15

16

August

17

18

19

20

August

21

22

23

August

24

25

26

27

August

28

29

30

31

September

SAPPHIRE FOR
CLEAR THINKING

"It was a September evening
and all the gaps and clearings
in the woods were brimmed
up with ruby sunset light."
–*Anne of Green Gables*

September

1

2

3

4

September

5

6

7

8

September

9
_____

_____

_____

10
_____

_____

_____

11
_____

_____

_____

September

12   Taryn's

13

14

15

September

16

17

18

19

September

20

21

22

September

23
_____

_____

_____

24
_____

_____

_____

25
_____

_____

_____

26
_____

_____

_____

_____

September

27

28

29

30

October

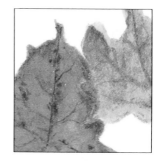

OPAL AND TOURMALINE
FOR HOPE

" 'I'm so glad I live in a world
where there are Octobers. It
would be terrible if we just
skipped from September to
November, wouldn't it?' "
–*Anne of Green Gables*

October

1

2

3 Steven

4